Easy Mongolian Cookbook

Enjoy Authentic Mongolian Cooking with
50 Delicious Mongolian Recipes

By
BookSumo Press
All rights reserved

Published by
http://www.booksumo.com

ENJOY THE RECIPES?
KEEP ON COOKING WITH 6 MORE FREE COOKBOOKS!

Click the link below and simply enter your email address to join the club and receive your 6 cookbooks.

http://booksumo.com/magnet

https://www.instagram.com/booksumopress/

https://www.facebook.com/booksumo/

LEGAL NOTES

All Rights Reserved. No Part Of This Book May Be Reproduced Or Transmitted In Any Form Or By Any Means. Photocopying, Posting Online, And / Or Digital Copying Is Strictly Prohibited Unless Written Permission Is Granted By The Book's Publishing Company. Limited Use Of The Book's Text Is Permitted For Use In Reviews Written For The Public.

Table of Contents

Traditional Mongolian Beef 7

Lamb from Mongolia 8

Mongolian Vegetables and Meatballs 9

Mongolian Flank Steak Bowls 10

Sweet Garlic Sriracha Steak 11

Meatballs Mongolian with Sweet Chili Sauce and Peanuts 12

Mongolian Lamb Skillet 13

Kebabs Mongolian 14

Chicken Breasts with Plum Sauce, and Peanut Honey 15

Mongolian Crock Pot Beef 16

How to Make a Mongolian Style Sauce for Rice and Meats 17

Spicy Pomegranate Marinade 18

Mongolian Basmati 19

Mongolian Sirloin with Vegetables 20

Spicy Peanut Butter Dip 21

Chicken Mongol 22

Mongolian Ground Beef Salad 23

Mongolian Marinade II 24

Mongolian Pot Pie 25

Mongolian Lunch Box Salad 26

Traditional Noodle Stir-Fry 27

Vegetarian Mongolian Sampler 28

Heart of Mongolian Smoothie 29

Sweet Ginger Meatballs 30

Mongolian Lamb 31

Sweet Tofu Oriental 32

Thursday's 30-Minute Beef Oriental 33

Mongolian Potluck 34

Beef Bok Choy 35

Mongolian Paella 36

Mongolian Lettuce Cups 37

Mongolian Dump Dinner 38

Mongolian Lamb Dumb Dinner 39

Mongolian Wontons 40

Mongolian Beef and Asparagus 41

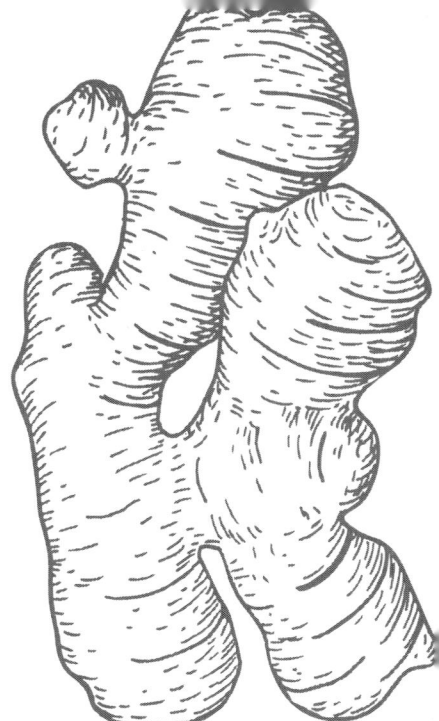

10-Ingredient Mongolian Dinner 42

Mr. Wong's Secret Beef 43

Classic Grilled Teriyaki Salmon 44

Tasty Beef Meatballs 45

Mongolian Potato Quarters 46

Glazed Swordfish 47

Tipsy Mahi Mahi Teriyaki With Fruity Jalapeno Salsa 48

Mongolian Teriyaki Meat 49

Oriental Tuna Steaks 50

Chicken Kabobs II 51

Tilapia Fillets with Teriyaki Sauce 52

Glazed Salmon Fillets with Orzo 53

Mongolian Burgers 54

Traditional Mongolian Beef

Prep Time: 10 mins
Total Time: 30 mins

Servings per Recipe: 2
Calories 847.3
Fat 23.4g
Cholesterol 154.2mg
Sodium 4175.5mg
Carbohydrates 103.0g
Protein 56.6g

Ingredients

2 tsp vegetable oil
1/2 tsp ginger, minced
1 tbsp garlic, chopped
1/2 C. soy sauce
1/2 C. water
3/4 C. dark brown sugar
vegetable oil, for frying (about 1 C.)

1 lb. flank steak
1/4 C. cornstarch
2 large green onions, sliced on the diagonal into one-inch lengths

Directions

1. For the sauce: in a medium pan, heat 2 tsp of the vegetable oil on medium-low heat and sauté the ginger and garlic with the soy sauce a little.
2. Then, stir in the water.
3. Add the brown sugar and stir till sugar is dissolved.
4. Increase the heat to medium and cook for about 2-3 minutes, stirring continuously.
5. Remove from the heat.
6. Cut the flank steak against the grain into 1/4-inch thick bite-size slices.
7. Coat the steak slices with the cornstarch slightly and keep aside for about 10 minutes.
8. In a wok, heat 1 C. of the oil on medium heat and sear the beef slices for about 2 minutes.
9. With a slotted spoon, transfer the beef onto paper towels lined plate to drain.
10. Remove the oil from the wok.
11. Return the beef in pan on heat and simmer for about 1 minute.
12. Stir in the sauce and cook for about 1 minute, stirring continuously.
13. Stir in the green onions and cook for about 1 minute, stirring continuously.
14. With a slotted spoon, transfer the beef mixture onto a serving plate.

LAMB
from Mongolia

Prep Time: 15 mins
Total Time: 30 mins

Servings per Recipe: 4
Calories 593.1
Fat 44.1g
Cholesterol 93.2mg
Sodium 825.0mg
Carbohydrates 7.1g
Protein 22.9g

Ingredients

40 ml oil
500 g lamb fillets, cut into thin strips
2 cloves garlic, crushed
4 spring onions
40 ml soy sauce
80 ml dry sherry
40 ml sweet chili sauce
2 tsp toasted sesame seeds

Directions

1. In a wok, heat half of the oil and stir fry the lamb in batches for about 3 minutes.
2. Transfer the lamb into a bowl.
3. In the same wok, heat remaining oil and sauté the garlic and spring onion for about 2 minutes.
4. transfer the garlic mixture into a small bowl.
5. In the same wok, add the sherry and sauces and bring to a boil.
6. Reduce the heat and simmer for about 3-4 minutes.
7. Stir in the lamb and garlic mixture and cook till heated through. and toss to coat with the sauce.
8. Serve with a sprinkling of the sesame seeds.

Mongolian Vegetables and Meatballs

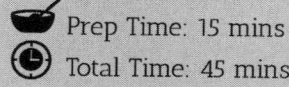

Prep Time: 15 mins
Total Time: 45 mins

Servings per Recipe: 4
Calories   623.5
Fat   17.9 g
Cholesterol   129.5 mg
Sodium   1215.5 mg
Carbohydrates   77.9 g
Protein   37.5 g

Ingredients

2 tsp cornstarch
3 tbsp soy sauce
2 tbsp red wine vinegar
2 tbsp hoisin sauce
1/4 tsp ground ginger
1/4 tsp garlic powder
1/4 tsp ground black pepper
1 egg, beaten
1/2 C. evaporated milk
1 C. breadcrumbs
1/2 tsp onion salt
1/4 tsp garlic powder
1/4 tsp ground black pepper
1 lb lean ground beef
1 C. corn kernel, cut from the cob
1 C. zucchini
1 C. red bell pepper
1/2 C. onion
2 C. cooked rice
1/2 tsp toasted sesame seeds
Foil

Directions

1. Set your oven to 350 degrees F before doing anything else.
2. In a small bowl, add the cornstarch, soy sauce, vinegar, hoisin sauce, ginger, garlic powder and pepper and beat till well combined.
3. In another large bowl, add the egg, evaporated milk, breadcrumbs, onion salt, garlic powder and black pepper and beat till well combined.
4. Crumble the beef over mixture and mix well.
5. Make 1-inch balls from the mixture.
6. Tear off 4 12-inch pieces of foil and arrange on to a smooth surface.
7. Place 1/4 of the vegetables in the center of each foil piece and top with 1/4 of the meatballs and 1/4 of the sauce.
8. Carefully, fold each foil piece over the mixture and crimp edges to make packets.
9. Arrange the packets onto a baking sheet.
10. Cook in the oven for about 30 minutes.
11. Divide rice onto serving plates and top each plate with 1 packet mixture.
12. Serve with a sprinkling of the sesame seeds.

MONGOLIAN
Flank Steak Bowls

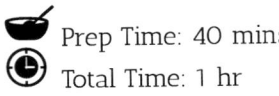 Prep Time: 40 mins
Total Time: 1 hr

Servings per Recipe: 6
Calories 302.4
Fat 10.5g
Cholesterol 39.0mg
Sodium 1411.7mg
Carbohydrates 32.7g
Protein 19.7g

Ingredients

1/4 C. broth
2 1/2 tbsp ginger root, finely grated
2 tbsp soy sauce
2 tbsp peanut oil
1 tbsp brown sugar
1 tbsp cornstarch
2 large garlic cloves, crushed
1/2 tsp red pepper flakes
12 oz. flank steaks, very thinly sliced across the grain and cut into 1 1/2-inch lengths
1 lb. bok choy, thinly sliced crosswise
3 1/2 oz. fresh shiitake mushrooms, wiped, stems removed, and thinly sliced
4 large scallions, thinly sliced
2 medium carrots, peeled and cut into 1/4 inch slices
4 C. beef stock
2 C. water
1/3 C. hoisin sauce
4 oz. soba noodles
Chinese hot pepper oil, to taste

Directions

1. In a resealable plastic bag, add the beef, sherry, soy sauce, 1 tbsp of the oil, brown ginger, garlic, sugar, corn starch and red pepper flakes and seal it.
2. Shake the bag to coat completely and keep aside in room temperature for about 30 minutes.
3. Remove the beef from the bag, reserving the marinade.
4. In a large wok, heat 1 tsp of the oil on high heat and stir fry the beef for about 1-2 minutes.
5. Transfer th beef into a bowl and keep aside.
6. In the same wok, add the remaining oil and stir-fry the mushrooms, carrots, bok choy and scallions for about 1-2 minutes.
7. Stir in the reserved marinade, hoisin sauce, stock and water and bring to a boil.
8. Stir in the noodles and simmer for about 8-10 minutes.
9. Stir in the beef and cook till heated through.
10. Stir in a few drops of the Chinese hot pepper oil and serve immediately.

Sweet Garlic Sriracha Steak

Prep Time: 30 mins
Total Time: 45 mins

Servings per Recipe: 6
Calories	267.8
Fat	14.3g
Cholesterol	77.4mg
Sodium	520.4mg
Carbohydrates	8.5g
Protein	24.9g

Ingredients

- 1/4 C. hoisin sauce
- 1/4 C. low sodium chicken broth
- 2 tbsp rice vinegar
- 2 tbsp chopped garlic
- 2 tbsp toasted sesame oil
- 1 tbsp brown sugar
- 1 tbsp low sodium soy sauce
- 1 tbsp chopped fresh ginger
- 1 tsp Sriracha sauce
- 1 1/2 lb. flank steaks
- 1/2 tsp salt
- 1/2 tsp black pepper

Directions

1. In a food processor, add the hoisin sauce, Sriracha, vinegar, broth, sesame oil, brown sugar, soy sauce, garlic and ginger and pulse till smooth.
2. Score a diamond pattern over one side of steak.
3. In a resealable plastic bag, add the steak and sauce.
4. Seal the bag and shake to coat.
5. Keep aside in the room temperature for at least 20 minutes.
6. Set your grill to high and grease the grill grate.
7. Remove steak from the bag and season with the salt and pepper.
8. Arrange the steak onto grill and cook, covered for about 5 minutes.
9. Flip and cook till desired doneness.
10. Transfer the steak onto cutting board and keep aside for about 5 minutes before slicing.
11. Cut the steak against the grain into thin slices and serve..

MEATBALLS MONGOLIAN with Sweet Chili Sauce and Peanuts

 Prep Time: 1 hr 15 mins
Total Time: 1 hr 40 mins

Servings per Recipe: 4
Calories 596.3
Fat 44.0g
Cholesterol 137.8mg
Sodium 408.2mg
Carbohydrates 21.8g
Protein 27.6g

Ingredients

500 g ground lamb
1 tsp grated fresh ginger
2 garlic cloves, crushed
1 small onion, chopped
50 g stale breadcrumbs
2 tsp broth
2 tsp soy sauce
1 tbsp chopped parsley
1 egg
2 tbsp vegetable oil
1 large red bell pepper, sliced
4 green shallots, sliced
1 lamb stock cube
1 tsp cornflour
250 ml water
2 tsp hoisin sauce
2 tsp sweet chili sauce
1 tsp peanut butter
1/2 tsp five-spice powder
40 g unsalted dry roasted peanuts

Directions

1. In a bowl, mix together the lamb, onion, ginger, garlic, parsley, breadcrumbs, soy sauce, broth and egg.
2. With 1 tbsp of the mixture, make balls.
3. Arrange the balls onto a tray and refrigerate for about 1 hour.
4. In a wok, heat the oil and stir fry the meatballs in batches till cooked through.
5. Transfer the meatballs onto plate.
6. In the same wok, add the pepper and shallot and stir fry till tender.
7. Add the meatballs and remaining ingredients except peanuts and cook till mixture becomes thick, stirring continuously.
8. Serve with a sprinkling of the peanuts.

Mongolian Lamb Skillet

Prep Time: 20 mins
Total Time: 35 mins

Servings per Recipe: 4
Calories 766.0
Fat 29.1g
Cholesterol 90.0mg
Sodium 379.0mg
Carbohydrates 92.4g
Protein 30.5g

Ingredients

1 tsp cornflour
1 tbsp soy sauce (salt-reduced)
1 tbsp rice wine vinegar
2 tsp black bean sauce
1/2 tsp Chinese five spice powder
1 tsp olive oil
500 g lamb steaks (leg trimmed of fat and cut across the grain into strips)
1 brown onion (cut into wedges)
100 g button mushrooms (sliced)
2 celery ribs (thinly sliced diagonally)
1 zucchini (large halved lengthwise, thinly sliced)
3 carrots (Halved lengthwise thinly sliced)
1/4 Chinese cabbage (shredded)
2 garlic cloves (minced)
1 tsp ginger (fresh finely grated)
2 tbsp water
210 g rice (1 C.)

Directions

1. In a bowl, add the cornflour, soy sauce, vinegar, black bean sauce and five spice powder and mix well.
2. Grease a large wok with a little oil and heat on high heat.
3. Add the lamb in batches and stir fry for about 2 minutes.
4. Transfer the lamb onto a plate.
5. Grease the same wok with some oil and heat on medium-high heat.
6. Add the onion, mushroom, celery, zucchini, carrot, cabbage, ginger and garlic and stir fry for about 2 minutes.
7. Add the water and cook, covered for about 2 minutes, tossing twice.
8. Add the lamb and sauce and toss till heated through.
9. Divide the rice onto serving plates and serve with a topping of the lamb mixture.

KEBABS
Mongolian

Prep Time: 15 mins
Total Time: 30 mins

Servings per Recipe: 1
Calories	84.1
Fat	4.7g
Cholesterol	24.2mg
Sodium	146.6mg
Carbohydrates	1.9g
Protein	7.7g

Ingredients

2 1/2 lb. flank steaks
1/2 C. hoisin sauce
2 tbsp peanut oil
2 tbsp sesame oil
2 tbsp broth
2 tbsp soy sauce

1/2 tsp sugar
1/2 tsp pepper
1/2 tsp fresh ginger, grated
1 garlic clove, crushed

Directions

1. Cut the steak across grain into 1/8-inch thick strips diagonally.
2. In a large heavy-duty zip lock plastic bag, add the beef and remaining all ingredients.
3. Seal the bag and shake to coat.
4. Refrigerator for 8 hours, flipping occasionally.
5. Meanwhile, soak the 32 (6-inch) wooden skewers in water for at least 10 minutes.
6. Set the broiler of your oven and arrange oven rack about 3-inch from the heating element.
7. Thread steak onto pre-soaked skewers.
8. Cook under the broiler for about 2-3 minutes per side.

Chicken Breasts with Plum Sauce, and Peanut Honey

Prep Time: 20 mins
Total Time: 50 mins

Servings per Recipe: 4
Calories 809.4
Fat 36.6g
Cholesterol 162.9mg
Sodium 899.6mg
Carbohydrates 61.8g
Protein 56.2g

Ingredients

For the Meat
3/4 tbsp ginger, peeled and minced
3 garlic cloves, minced
1 shallot, peeled and minced
1 tbsp cilantro leaf, roughly chopped
1/4 C. Spanish sherry wine vinegar
1/8 C. hoisin sauce
1 1/2 tbsp soy sauce
1 1/2 tbsp rice wine vinegar
1 1/2 tbsp sesame oil
1 1/2 tbsp plum sauce
1 1/2 tbsp creamy peanut butter
1 1/2 tbsp honey
1 1/2 tsp salsa, sriracha
4 (8 -10 oz.) chicken breasts, with one small wing bone attached
For the Rice
1 C. raw long grain rice
2 tbsp annatto oil
2 tbsp butter
4 garlic cloves, peeled and minced
1 scotch bonnet pepper, stem and seeds discarded and minced
1/2 onion, diced medium small
1 carrot, peeled and diced med. small
1 stalk celery, cleaned and diced med. small
2 small bay leaves, broken
salt and pepper, to taste
1 1/4 C. chicken stock

Directions

1. In a large bowl, add the chicken and all marinade ingredients and mix well.
2. Refrigerate, covered for about 1-3 hours.
3. For the rice: in a pan, heat the prepared annatto oil and butter on medium-high heat and sauté the scotch bonnet and garlic for about 15 seconds.
4. Stir in the remaining vegetables and bay leaves and cook for about 10 minutes, stirring frequently.
5. Add the rice, salt and pepper and stir to combine.
6. Stir in the chicken stock and bring to a boil.
7. Immediately, reduce the heat to very low and simmer, covered for about 13-15 minutes.
8. Meanwhile, cook the chicken breasts onto grill till cooked completely.
9. Serve chicken breasts alongside the rice.

MONGOLIAN
Crock Pot Beef

 Prep Time: 10 mins
Total Time: 6 hr 10 mins

Servings per Recipe: 2
Calories   1270.9
Fat   45.4g
Cholesterol   275.5mg
Sodium   6266.9mg
Carbohydrates   107.3g
Protein   106.1g

Ingredients

1 1/2 lb. beef flank steak, cut into stir-fry sized strips
1/4 C. cornstarch
2 tbsp olive oil
1/2 tsp minced ginger
2 garlic cloves, minced

3/4 C. soy sauce
3/4 C. water
3/4 C. brown sugar
1/2 C. shredded carrot
3 medium green onions, chopped

Directions

1. Grease a slow cooker with non-stick cooking spray.
2. Coat each piece of steak with the cornstarch evenly and transfer into a crock pot.
3. In a bowl, add the remaining ingredients and mix well.
4. Place the mixture over beef.
5. Set the crock pot on High and cook, covered for about 2-3 hours.

How to Make a Mongolian Style Sauce for Rice and Meats

Prep Time: 15 mins
Total Time: 15 mins

Servings per Recipe: 1
Calories	475.5
Fat	16.3g
Cholesterol	3.0mg
Sodium	3590.2mg
Carbohydrates	76.8g
Protein	6.0g

Ingredients

- 4 C. hoisin sauce
- 2 C. plum sauce
- 1 C. oyster sauce
- 1/2 C. soy sauce
- 1/2 C. Chinese sweet black vinegar
- 1 C. shaoxing wine
- 1/2 C. peanut oil
- 1/2 C. chili oil
- 1 tbsp sesame oil
- 1 tbsp dried orange peel
- 2 tbsp minced garlic
- 3 tbsp minced ginger
- 1 tbsp onion powder

Directions

1. In a bowl, mix together all the ingredients.
2. Place in a glass jar and refrigerator overnight before using.

SPICY Pomegranate Marinade

 Prep Time: 5 mins
Total Time: 20 mins

Servings per Recipe: 1
Calories	466.0
Fat	28.5g
Cholesterol	0.0mg
Sodium	2085.6mg
Carbohydrates	52.7g
Protein	5.2g

Ingredients

- 1 tsp chili powder
- 2 tbsp dark soy sauce
- 2 tsp ground cumin
- 2 tbsp olive oil
- 1/2 lemon, juiced
- 3 tbsp pomegranate molasses

Directions

1. In a bowl, mix together all the ingredients.
2. Add the lamb and coat with marinade generously.
3. Refrigerator overnight before cooking.

Mongolian Basmati

Prep Time: 10 mins
Total Time: 20 mins

Servings per Recipe: 3
Calories	488.2
Fat	19.5g
Cholesterol	0.0mg
Sodium	1426.4mg
Carbohydrates	64.6g
Protein	16.2g

Ingredients

- 1/4 C. tamari
- 1 tbsp brown sugar
- 1 tbsp garlic, minced
- 1 tbsp ginger, minced
- 1 tsp hoisin sauce
- 1 tbsp sesame oil
- 1 tbsp water
- 1/2 lb. firm tofu
- 2 tbsp peanut oil
- 1/2 medium yellow onion, sliced
- 2 large carrots, sliced
- 1 green onion
- 1 C. basmati rice
- 2 C. water

Directions

1. Chop the tofu in medium strips.
2. In a baking dish, mix together the tamari, brown sugar, garlic, ginger, Hoisin sauce, sesame oil and water.
3. Add the tofu and coat with the marinade generously.
4. Refrigerate, covered for about 1/2-1 hour.
5. Prepare the rice according to package's directions.
6. In a frying pan, heat the peanut oil on medium heat and sauté the onion and carrots till onion is translucent.
7. Add the beef and sauce and stir fry for about 5-10 minutes.
8. Serve alongside the rice with a topping of the chopped green onion.

MONGOLIAN SIRLOIN
with Vegetables

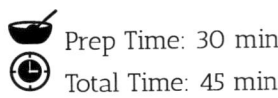

Prep Time: 30 mins
Total Time: 45 mins

Servings per Recipe: 6
Calories 568.5
Fat 28.3g
Cholesterol 114.6mg
Sodium 1688.5mg
Carbohydrates 43.0g
Protein 35.6g

Ingredients

2 lb. sirloin steaks, sliced into 1/4 inch pieces
1 tsp salt
1 tbsp sugar
1 tbsp garlic powder
1 tbsp onion powder
1 tbsp ginger powder
1 tsp baking soda
3 tbsp broth
2 tbsp cornstarch
3 tbsp oil
1 C. baby corn, 1/4 inch strips
1 C. red onion, 1/4 inch strips
2 C. leeks, 1/4 inch strips
1 C. jicama, 1/4 inch strips
1 C. green pepper, 1/4 inch strips
1 C. carrot, 1/4 inch strips
1 C. hoisin sauce
2 C. beef stock
cornstarch paste
salt
white pepper
oil

Directions

1. In a large bowl, mix together the beef, salt, sugar, garlic, onion, ginger, baking soda, broth, cornstarch and oil and keep aside for about 30 minutes.
2. In a wok, heat 2 tbsp of the oil and stir fry the vegetable for about 1 minute.
3. Transfer the vegetables into a warm plate.
4. In the same wok, heat 1/3 C. of the oil on high heat and stir fry the beef and hoisin sauce for about 2-3 minutes.
5. Add the beef stock and bring to a boil.
6. Stir in the cornstarch roux and cook till thickened.
7. Stir in the vegetables, salt and pepper and remove from the heat.

Spicy Peanut Butter Dip

Prep Time: 5 mins
Total Time: 5 mins

Servings per Recipe: 4
Calories   200.4
Fat   16.2g
Cholesterol   0.0mg
Sodium   399.8mg
Carbohydrates   8.6g
Protein   8.5g

Ingredients

1/2 C. peanut butter
1 tbsp light soy sauce
1 tbsp chili bean paste
2 tsp sugar
1/4 C. hot water
fresh cilantro

Directions

1. In a bowl, add the peanut butter, soy sauce, chili bean paste, sugar and hot water and beat till well combined.
2. Divide the sauce into 4 small serving bowls and top with the chopped cilantro before serving.

CHICKEN Mongol

 Prep Time: 1 hr 10 mins
Total Time: 1 hr 20 mins

Servings per Recipe: 4
Calories	457.5
Fat	32.8g
Cholesterol	118.4mg
Sodium	942.6mg
Carbohydrates	12.5g
Protein	25.6g

Ingredients

6 chicken thighs, boneless, slice 1/2 inch
1 tsp garlic, minced
1 tbsp oyster sauce
1 tsp soy sauce
1 tbsp rice wine
1 tsp sesame oil
1 tsp salt
1/2 tsp white pepper
1/2 tsp red chili pepper
1 tsp sugar
1/2 tsp baking powder
2 tbsp cornstarch
4 tbsp flour
3 tbsp peanut oil
2 stalks green onions, minced

Directions

1. In a bowl, add all the ingredients except the oil and green onion and mix well.
2. Refrigerate to marinade for about 1 hour.
3. In a large nonstick skillet, heat 3 tbsp of the oil and stir fry the chicken till golden brown from both sides.
4. Serve hot with a garnishing of the green onion.

Mongolian Ground Beef Salad

Prep Time: 15 mins
Total Time: 40 mins

Servings per Recipe: 4
Calories   147.5
Fat   9.1g
Cholesterol   38.5mg
Sodium   591.3mg
Carbohydrates   4.1g
Protein   11.7g

Ingredients

- 4 C. lettuce, coarsely torn
- 1 tbsp ginger, minced
- 1 tbsp garlic, minced
- 1/2 lb ground beef
- 1/2 tsp salt
- 1 tbsp soy sauce
- 1 tbsp rice vinegar
- 1/2 C. warm water
- 2 tsp cornstarch
- 1 tbsp cold water
- 1/2 tsp toasted sesame oil

Directions

1. In a heavy skillet, heat the oil on medium-high heat and sauté the garlic for about 10 seconds.
2. Add the ginger and sauté till slightly softened.
3. Add the meat and salt cook till browned, breaking the lumps.
4. Stir in the soy sauce, vinegar and warm water and bring to a boil.
5. In a small bowl, dissolve the cornstarch in the cold water.
6. Add the cornstarch mixture into skillet and stir to combine well.
7. Stir in the sesame oil and remove from the heat.
8. in a wide salad bowl, place the lettuce.
9. Immediately, pour the hot sauce and toss to coat.
10. Serve immediately.

MONGOLIAN
Marinade II

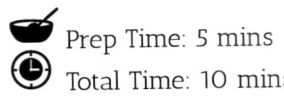
Prep Time: 5 mins
Total Time: 10 mins

Servings per Recipe: 4
Calories   87.6
Fat   1.1g
Cholesterol   0.0mg
Sodium   2016.1mg
Carbohydrates   16.3g
Protein   3.9g

Ingredients

1 tsp olive oil
1/2 tsp ginger powder
1 tbsp minced garlic
1/2 C. soy sauce
1/2 C. water
1/4 C. brown sugar

Directions

1. In a pan, heat the oil and sauté the ginger and garlic till aromatic.
2. Add the water, soy sauce and sugar and cook till sugar dissolves, stirring continuously.
3. Bring to a boil and reduce the heat to low.
4. Simmer till the desired thickness of the sauce.

Mongolian Pot Pie

Prep Time: 1 hr 30 mins
Total Time: 2 hr 5 mins

Servings per Recipe: 4
Calories   394.4
Fat   22.2g
Cholesterol   92.7mg
Sodium   1121.5mg
Carbohydrates   19.0g
Protein   27.4g

Ingredients

- 1/4 C. soy sauce
- 3 tbsp rice wine
- 1 tbsp sesame oil
- 1 tsp hoisin sauce
- 2 tbsp brown sugar
- 1 tbsp cornstarch
- 2 tsp ginger
- 2 garlic cloves
- 1 lb sirloin steak, strips
- 1 tbsp butter
- 1 garlic clove
- 4 oz. shiitake mushrooms
- 2 green onions with tops, diced
- 1 (13 7/8 oz.) cans pizza crusts
- 1/2 lb green beans
- 1 tbsp sesame seeds
- 1 egg
- 1 tbsp water

Directions

1. In a large bowl, mix together the soy sauce, wine, sesame oil, hoisin sauce, brown sugar, cornstarch, ginger and garlic.
2. Add the steak strips and coat with the marinade generously.
3. Refrigerate for at least 1 hour.
4. In a skillet, melt the butter and sautée the onions and mushrooms for about 3-4 minutes.
5. Unroll the pizza dough and cut into 4 rectangles.
6. Place about 2 tbsp of the mushroom mixture in the center of each rectangle.
7. Pull 4 corners of the dough together and twist to seal.
8. Set your oven to 350 degrees F and grease 4 ramekins.
9. In a pan, add 1 C. of the water and bring to a boil.
10. Add the green beans and cook, covered for about 3-4 minutes.
11. Drain well.
12. Remove the steak from the bowl, reserving marinade.
13. In a pan, add the reserved marinade and cook till sauce becomes thick.
14. Stir in the steak, green beans and sesame seed and remove from the heat.
15. Place the mixture into the prepared ramekins.
16. place the filled dough bundles on top of the steak mixture.
17. In a small bowl, add the egg and water and beat well.
18. Coat the top of dough with the egg mixture.
19. Cook in the oven for about 30-35 minutes.

MONGOLIAN
Lunch Box Salad

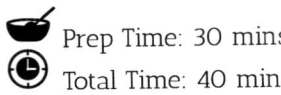 Prep Time: 30 mins
Total Time: 40 mins

Servings per Recipe: 4
Calories	1057.7
Fat	74.2g
Cholesterol	227.9mg
Sodium	732.1mg
Carbohydrates	28.0g
Protein	67.7g

Ingredients

FOR MARINADE
1 C. fresh orange juice
1/4 C. grated orange zest
1/4 C. honey
2 tbsp soy sauce
2 tsp chopped.peeled fresh ginger
2 tsp minced garlic
1/4 tsp dried red pepper flakes
4 (3/4 lb.) boneless beef top loin steaks, fat trimmed
DRESSING
2 tbsp red wine vinegar
1 tbsp Dijon mustard
1 tbsp chopped fresh tarragon or 1 tsp dried tarragon, crumbled
1 tbsp chopped shallots or 1 tbsp green onion
1/2 tsp minced garlic
1/2 C. olive oil
salt & freshly ground black pepper
assorted mixed greens, such as boston lettuce, oak lealettuce, and mustard greens, torn into bite-sized pieces

Directions

1. For the marinade: in a large shallow glass baking dish, mix together all the ingredients well.
2. Cover and keep aside in the room temperature for about 1 hour.
3. For the dressing: in a bowl, add the vinegar, mustard, tarragon, shallots, garlic, slat and pepper and beat till well combined.
4. Add the oil in slow steady stream and beat well. season to taste with.
5. Set your barbecue to high heat.
6. Remove steaks from the baking dish, reserving the marinade.
7. Cook the steaks on grill for about 5 minutes per side, basting with the reserved marinade occasionally.
8. Remove from the grill and cut the steaks into thin slices.
9. In a large bowl, add the greens and enough dressing and toss to coat.
10. Divide greens onto serving plates and top with the steak slices.
11. Serve immediately with any extra dressing.

Traditional Noodle Stir-Fry

Prep Time: 35 mins
Total Time: 35 mins

Servings per Recipe: 4
Calories   347.2
Fat   1.4g
Cholesterol   0.0mg
Sodium   2515.8mg
Carbohydrates 66.2g
Protein   18.1g

Ingredients

300 g udon noodles, uncooked
1/3 C. water
20 ml grated fresh ginger
2 tsp garlic, minced fresh
1 bunch green onion, cut into 1/2-inch pieces
120 g fresh shiitake mushrooms, stemmed & sliced
4 C. vegetable broth
1/4 C. soy sauce
1/2 tsp sambal oelek (ground fresh chili paste)
315 g lite silken extra firm tofu, cut into cubes
4 C. bok choy, sliced, stalks removed
1/3 C. cilantro, chopped

Directions

1. In a large pan of the lightly salted boiling water, cook the egg noodles for about 8-10 minutes.
2. Drain well and keep aside.
3. Meanwhile in a large pan, add 1/3 C. of the water, ginger and garlic and cook for about 2 minutes, stirring continuously.
4. Add the onions and mushrooms and cook for about 3 minutes.
5. Add the broth, soy sauce and chili paste and bring to a boil.
6. Add the tofu and bok choy and cook for about 2 minutes.
7. Remove from the heat and and stir in the cooked noodles and cilantro.
8. Serve immediately.

VEGETARIAN Mongolian Sampler

Prep Time: 20 mins
Total Time: 30 mins

Servings per Recipe: 2
Calories   512.0
Fat   16.2g
Cholesterol   0.9mg
Sodium   1036.8mg
Carbohydrates   81.6g
Protein   10.9g

Ingredients

1/4 C. hoisin sauce
1/4 C. water
1 tbsp Agave
1 tbsp soy sauce
1 tsp lemon juice
1 - 2 tsp chili-garlic sauce
2 tbsp canola oil
8 oz. shiitake mushrooms, stemmed and sliced
8 oz. seitan, cut into thin strips
2 tsp fresh ginger, grated
1/8 tsp ground cinnamon
1/8 tsp ground cloves
4 oz. snow peas, strings removed
2 scallions, trimmed and thinly sliced
1/4 C. chopped fresh cilantro
2 C. cooked rice, for serving

Directions

1. For the sauce: in a bowl, add the hoisin sauce, water, Agave, soy sauce, lemon juice and chili-garlic sauce and beat till well combined.
2. In a large skillet, heat the oil on medium-high heat and stir fry the mushrooms and seitan till lightly browned.
3. Add the ginger, cinnamon and cloves and cook for a few more minutes.
4. Add the sauce and snow peas and stir to combine.
5. Reduce the heat to medium and cook till the sauce becomes thick.
6. Remove from the heat and stir in the scallions and cilantro.
7. Serve over the rice.

Heart of Mongolian Smoothie

Prep Time: 10 mins
Total Time: 10 mins

Servings per Recipe: 4
Calories	52 kcal
Fat	0.2 g
Carbohydrates	12.5g
Protein	0.7 g
Cholesterol	0 mg
Sodium	3 mg

Ingredients

- 1 C. chopped fresh strawberries
- 1 C. orange juice
- 10 cubes ice
- 1 tbsp sugar

Directions

1. In a blender, add all the ingredients and pulse till smooth.
2. Transfer into glasses and serve immediately.

SWEET GINGER
Meatballs

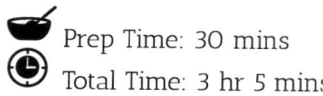

Prep Time: 30 mins
Total Time: 3 hr 5 mins

Servings per Recipe: 12
Calories 181 kcal
Fat 8.6 g
Carbohydrates 15.6 g
Protein 11.7 g
Cholesterol 37 mg
Sodium 519 mg

Ingredients

Mongolian Sauce:
1/2 C. hoisin sauce
4 cloves garlic, minced
2 tbsp red wine vinegar
1 1/2 tbsp soy sauce
1 tbsp grated fresh ginger
1 tbsp rice vinegar
2 tsp sesame oil
2 tsp white sugar
1 1/2 tsp hot sauce
1/2 tsp ground white pepper
1/2 tsp ground black pepper
Meatballs:
1 lb. ground beef
1/2 lb. ground lamb
1/2 head cabbage, chopped
1 yellow onion, chopped
1/2 C. panko bread crumbs
1/2 C. grated carrot
1 tbsp ground ginger
1/4 C. chopped green onion
6 cloves garlic, chopped
1 tsp garlic salt
1/2 tsp ground black pepper

Directions

1. Set your oven to 350 degrees F before doing anything else.
2. For the sauce: in a bowl, add the hoisin sauce, 4 garlic cloves, ginger, red wine vinegar, soy sauce, rice vinegar, sesame oil, sugar, hot sauce, white pepper, and black pepper and beat till well combined.
3. In another bowl, add all meatballs ingredients and 2 tbsp of the hoisin sauce mixture and mix till well combined.
4. Make meatballs from the mixture and arrange onto a jelly roll pan.
5. Cook in the oven for about 25 minutes.
6. Now, set your oven to broiler.
7. Flip the meatballs and cook under the broiler for about 10 minutes.
8. Transfer the warm meatballs into a slow cooker and top with the hoisin sauce mixture.
9. Set the slow cooker on Low and cook, covered for about 24 hours, stirring occasionally.

Mongolian Lamb

Prep Time: 15 mins
Total Time: 9 hr

Servings per Recipe: 10
Calories	325 kcal
Fat	17.7 g
Carbohydrates	13.3g
Protein	27 g
Cholesterol	93 mg
Sodium	688 mg

Ingredients

- 2/3 C. hoisin sauce
- 6 tbsp rice vinegar
- 1/2 C. minced green onions
- 1/4 C. mushroom soy sauce
- 4 tbsp minced garlic
- 2 tbsp honey
- 1/2 tsp sesame oil
- 1 tbsp toasted sesame seeds
- 1/2 tsp ground white pepper
- 1/2 tsp freshly ground black pepper
- 1 (5 lb.) boneless leg of lamb

Directions

1. In a large resealable plastic bag, add all the ingredients.
2. Seal the bag and shake to coat.
3. Refrigerate for 8 hours or overnight.
4. Set your grill to high heat and grease the grill grate.
5. Cook the lamb on the grill for about 15 minutes per side.
6. Transfer the lamb onto a serving platter and keep aside for about 20 minutes before slicing.

SWEET TOFU
Oriental

Prep Time: 40 mins
Total Time: 50 mins

Servings per Recipe: 6
Calories   378.1
Fat   12.4g
Cholesterol   0.0mg
Sodium   1454.7mg
Carbohydrates   57.5g
Protein   13.5g

Ingredients

3 tbsp sesame oil
1 tsp fresh ginger, minced
2 tbsp garlic, chopped
1 C. low sodium soy sauce
1 C. water
1 1/4 C. dark brown sugar
2 (14 oz.) containers extra firm tofu, pressed and pat dried
1/4 C. cornstarch
4 large green onions, cut into 1-2-inch slices
1 large red bell pepper, cut in to long slices lengthwise (optional)
10 oz. mushrooms, quartered (optional)

Directions

1. Cut the tofu in half lengthwise and then cut in 1-inch long and about 3/4-inch wide pieces.
2. In a deep skillet, heat the sesame oil on medium-low heat and sauté the ginger and garlic for about 30 seconds.
3. Add he brown sugar, soy sauce and water and cook till the sugar is dissolved.
4. Increase the heat to medium high and boil sauce for about 3 minutes.
5. Remove from the heat and keep aside to cool slightly.
6. Add the tofu strips inside the sauce and refrigerate to marinate them for about 30-60 minutes.
7. through a colander, strain the liquid from the tofu and reserve in a bowl.
8. In the reserves tofu liquid, add the cornstarch and stir till dissolved.
9. In a skillet, heat a little of the sesame oil on medium heat and cook the tofu pieces till golden brown.
10. Add green onions, peppers, mushrooms and sauce and cook till heated through.

Thursday's 30-Minute Beef Oriental

Prep Time: 15 mins
Total Time: 30 mins

Servings per Recipe: 2
Calories   5207.7
Fat   541.6g
Cholesterol   140.3mg
Sodium   2053.0mg
Carbohydrates   86.1g
Protein   15.9g

Ingredients

10 oz. beef, sliced into 3/8-inch strips
1/4 C. cornstarch
4 C. vegetable oil
2 tsp vegetable oil
1/2 tsp chopped garlic
1 tsp rice wine vinegar
1/4 C. soy sauce
2/3 C. sugar
1/4 yellow onion, sliced
2 green onions, sliced
1/4 tsp white pepper
1/4 tsp sesame seed oil

Directions

1. Coat the beef with the cornstarch and keep aside for about 5 minutes.
2. In a deep skillet, heat 4 C. of the vegetable oil and fry beef till crispy.
3. Transfer the beef onto a plate.
4. In another skillet, heat 2 tsp of the vegetable oil and sauté the garlic, rice wine, soy sauce and beef well.
5. stir in the sugar and stir fry for about 1 minute.
6. Stir in the yellow onion, green onion and white pepper and stir well.
7. Stir in the sesame oil and serve.

MONGOLIAN
Potluck

Prep Time: 15 mins
Total Time: 30 mins

Servings per Recipe: 4
Calories   306.9
Fat   17.5g
Cholesterol   69.1mg
Sodium   838.3mg
Carbohydrates   10.0g
Protein   26.7g

Ingredients

1 tbsp soy sauce
1 tbsp cornstarch
2 garlic cloves, minced
1 lb. beef round steak, cut into thin strips
3/4 C. water
2 tbsp soy sauce
2 1/2 tsp cornstarch
1/2 tsp Splenda sugar substitute
2 tbsp diced red peppers
2 tbsp olive oil, divided
2 carrots, thinly sliced
1 bunch green onion, cut into 2 inch pieces (separate the white from the green)

Directions

1. In a bowl, mix together the beef strips, 1 tbsp of the soy sauce, 1 tbsp of the cornstarch and minced garlic.
2. Keep aside for at least 10 minutes.
3. In another bowl, mix together the water, 2 tbsp of the soy sauce, 2 1/2 tsp of the cornstarch, splenda and red pepper.
4. In a skillet, heat 1 tbsp of the olive oil on high heat and sear the beef for about 1 minute.
5. Transfer the beef onto a plate.
6. In the same skillet, heat remaining 1 tbsp of the olive oil and sauté the carrots and white part of green onions for about 2 minutes.
7. Stir in the green portion of the onion and sauté for about 1 minute.
8. Stir in the beef and sauce mixture and cook till sauce becomes thick.

Beef Bok Choy

Prep Time: 10 mins
Total Time: 15 mins

Servings per Recipe: 4
Calories   603.0
Fat   43.4g
Cholesterol   115.8mg
Sodium   1319.6mg
Carbohydrates   12.4g
Protein   40.7g

Ingredients

- 3 C. flank steaks, thinly sliced against the grain
- 1 C. shiitake mushroom, thinly sliced
- 1 C. bok choy
- 1 tbsp oyster sauce
- 1/2 C. vegetable oil
- 1/8 C. fresh ginger
- 2 cloves finely chopped garlic
- 1/2 tbsp sesame oil
- 1/4 C. light soy sauce
- 1/3 C. chicken broth

Directions

1. In a bowl, mix together the flank steak, oyster sauce and 1/4 C. f the vegetable oil.
2. In another bowl, mix together the soy sauce, sesame oil and chicken broth.
3. In a hot wok, heat the remaining vegetable oil and sauté the garlic and ginger till aromatic.
4. Add the flank steak and sauté for about 2 minutes.
5. Add the mushroom and bok choy and sauté for about 2 minutes.
6. Add the soy sauce and cook for about 30 seconds.

MONGOLIAN
Paella

Prep Time: 12 mins
Total Time: 24 mins

Servings per Recipe: 4
Calories 264.4
Fat 7.3g
Cholesterol 39.2mg
Sodium 1415.3mg
Carbohydrates 33.0g
Protein 17.1g

Ingredients

8 oz. flank steaks, sliced against the grain into 1/4-inch thick slices
2 tsp cornstarch
1 tsp sesame oil
salt and black pepper, to taste
SAUCE
2/3 C. water
1/3 C. low sodium soy sauce
1/3 C. hoisin sauce
1/3 C. Thai sweet chili sauce
2 garlic cloves, minced
1/2 tsp grated ginger
2 tbsp cornstarch
1/2 C. pineapple chunk
1/4 C. thinly sliced carrot
4 medium zucchini, cut into noodles
OPTIONAL GARNISH
green onion, sliced thinly
sesame seeds

Directions

1. In a large bowl, mix together the steak, salt, pepper, sesame oil and cornstarch.
2. Refrigerate to marinate for about 30 minutes.
3. In a medium bowl, add all the sauce ingredients and beat till well combined.
4. In a large skillet, heat 1 tbsp of the cooking oil on medium-high heat and sear the beef for about 1-2 minutes.
5. Transfer the beef onto a plate.
6. In the same skillet, add the pineapples and cook for about 5 minutes.
7. Stir in the cooked beef and carrots.
8. Add the zucchini noodles and toss to coat well.
9. Cook for about 1-2 minutes.
10. Serve immediately with a garnishing of the green onions and sesame seeds.

Mongolian Lettuce Cups

Prep Time: 20 mins
Total Time: 40 mins

Servings per Recipe: 4
Calories   899.0
Fat   84.4g
Cholesterol   112.7mg
Sodium   667.2mg
Carbohydrates   23.4g
Protein   12.0g

Ingredients

1 (5 1/3 oz.) packages dynasty saifun bean threads
1 chicken bouillon cube
4 tsp cornstarch
2 tbsp dynasty hoisin sauce
1 tbsp dynasty szechwan chili sauce
1 tbsp Kikkoman soy sauce
3 tsp vegetable oil, divided
1 lb lean tender beef, cut into 1/2 inch cubes
5 green onions with tops, cut into 1/2 inch lengths
1 (8 oz.) cans dynasty water chestnuts, drained and coarsely chopped
4 C. packed shredded iceberg lettuce

Directions

1. Soften 1 bundle of the saifun according to package's directions.
2. Drain well and rinse under running cold water and again, drain well. C
3. Chop the saifun roughly and keep aside.
4. In a large bowl, dissolve the bouillon in 1/2 C. of the boiling water.
5. Add 1/2 C. cold water, cornstarch, hoisin, chili and soy sauces and stir till cornstarch is dissolved.
6. In a large nonstick frying pan, heat 1 1/2 tsp of the oil on high heat and sear the beef in batches of pan for about 3 minutes.
7. Transfer the beef into a bowl.
8. Repeat with the remaining 1 1/2 tsp of the oil and beef.
9. Return all the beef into pan.
10. Add the green onions, water chestnuts, saifun and chili sauce mixture and cook for about 2 minutes.
11. Remove from the heat and serve over the bed of the lettuce.

MONGOLIAN
Dump Dinner

Prep Time: 10 mins
Total Time: 8 hr 10 mins

Servings per Recipe: 4
Calories 532.0
Fat 12.4g
Cholesterol 110.5mg
Sodium 3160.8mg
Carbohydrates 59.6g
Protein 42.7g

Ingredients

1 1/2-2 lb. London broil beef (cut into strips)
1/4 C. cornstarch
1 medium onion, sliced thinly
3 - 4 large carrots, sliced thickly
1/2 tsp ginger, minced

2 garlic cloves, minced
3/4 C. soy sauce
1/2 C. water
1/4 C. broth
3/4 C. brown sugar
1/4 tsp black pepper

Directions

1. Coat the beef strips with the cornstarch and keep aside.
2. In a crock pot, add the remaining ingredients and mix well.
3. Place beef strips over the mixture.
4. St the crock pot on Low and cook, covered for about 6-8 hours.

Mongolian Lamb Dumb Dinner

Prep Time: 2 hr
Total Time: 6 hr

Servings per Recipe: 6
Calories   286.6
Fat   16.3g
Cholesterol   112.6mg
Sodium   597.9mg
Carbohydrates   9.6g
Protein   24.2g

Ingredients

500 g lean lamb (boneless)
2 red onions (chopped)
1 oil, for cooking
1 egg (lightly whisk with fork)
2 tbsp soy sauce
2 tsp brown sugar
3 tsp corn flour
1/2 tsp bicarbonate of soda
1 tbsp garlic (crushed)
1 tbsp sweet chili sauce
1 tbsp hoisin sauce
1/2 tsp Chinese five spice herbs
1/2 tsp ginger (from jar)
1/2 fresh leek

Directions

1. In bowl, mix together the garlic, egg, soy sauce, sugar, corn flour and soda bicarbonate.
2. Add the lamb and coat with the marinade generously.
3. Refrigerate for about 2 hours or overnight.
4. For the sauce: in bowl mix together 2 tbsp of the water, chili sauce, hoisin sauce, Chinese five spice and ginger.
5. In a pan, heat the oil and sauté the onions till tender.
6. Add the lamb and sear till browned.
7. Transfer the lamb into a slow cooker and top with the sauce and leek.
8. Set the slow cooker on High and cook, covered for about 3-4 hours.

MONGOLIAN
Wontons

Prep Time: 15 mins
Total Time: 25 mins

Servings per Recipe: 2
Calories   432.4
Fat   27.2g
Cholesterol   85.8mg
Sodium   257.1mg
Carbohydrates   22.6g
Protein   22.7g

Ingredients

8 wonton wrappers
1/2 lb. ground lamb
1/3 C. onion, minced
1 tsp garlic, minced
2 tbsp fresh parsley, minced
1 jalapeño pepper, minced

sea salt and pepper
1 C. Greek yogurt, placed in a cheesecloth-lined sieve and drained overnight in the fridge
4 tsp dried mint

Directions

1. In a bowl, add the lamb, onion, garlic, parsley, jalapeño pepper, salt and black pepper ad mix well.
2. Refrigerate to chill completely.
3. Arrange the wrapper onto a smooth surface.
4. Place a tsp of the lamb mixture over each wrapper and fold to form a half circle, sealing with wet fingers.
5. Arrange the dumplings onto baking sheet dusted with the cornstarch.
6. In a pan of the rapidly boiling salted water, add the dumplings ans stir once.
7. Cook for about 2 minutes.
8. Transfer onto a paper towels lined plate to drain.
9. In a large sauté pan, add yogurt on medium heat and cook till warmed.
10. Add the hot dumplings and toss to coat well.
11. Divide the dumpling mixture into serving bowls and serve with a sprinkling of the dried mint.

Mongolian Beef and Asparagus

Prep Time: 1 hr 20 mins
Total Time: 1 hr 35 mins

Servings per Recipe: 4
Calories   393.9
Fat   23.7g
Cholesterol   46.8mg
Sodium   782.0mg
Carbohydrates 16.2g
Protein   29.5g

Ingredients

1 lb. flank steak
2 tbsp light soy sauce
3 tbsp hoisin sauce
1 tbsp rice wine
1 tbsp cornstarch
1 tsp sugar
1 1/2 lb. asparagus

4 tbsp peanut oil
1 clove garlic, minced
1 slice fresh ginger, minced
1/8 tsp crushed red pepper flakes

Directions

1. Slice the steak thinly and then, cut into 2-inch wide strips.
2. In a bowl, add the soy sauce, hoisin sauce, rice wine, cornstarch and sugar and mix well.
3. Add steak strips and coat wit marinade generously.
4. Refrigerate to marinate for about 1 hour.
5. In a pan of the boiling water, blanch the asparagus for about 5 minutes.
6. In a skillet, heat 2 tbsp of the oil and stir fry the asparagus for about 2 minutes.
7. Transfer the asparagus into a bowl.
8. In the same skillet, heat 2 tbsp of the oil and sauté the ginger, garlic and red pepper flakes for about 1 minute.
9. Add the beef strips and stir fry for about 3-4 minutes.

10-INGREDIENT
Mongolian Dinner

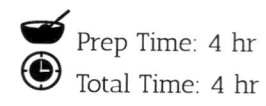

Prep Time: 4 hr
Total Time: 4 hr

Servings per Recipe: 4
Calories   421.9
Fat   11.7g
Cholesterol   46.4mg
Sodium   2092.0mg
Carbohydrates   51.1g
Protein   28.2g

Ingredients

1 lb. flank steak
1/4 C. cornstarch
2 tsp olive oil
1/2 tsp minced ginger
1 tbsp minced garlic
1/2 C. soy sauce

1/2 C. water
3/4 C. brown sugar
2 large green onions, chopped
1 C. cooked basmati rice

Directions

1. Cut the steak into bite size pieces and coat with the cornstarch evenly.
2. Keep aside for about 10 minutes.
3. In a skillet, heat the oil and sear for about 2-4 minutes.
4. Transfer the beef into a crock pot.
5. Add remaining ingredients and mix well.
6. Set the crock pot on Low and cook, covered for about 4 hours.
7. Enjoy with rice topped liberally with sauce from the crock pot.

Mr. Wong's Secret Beef

Prep Time: 45 mins
Total Time: 55 mins

Servings per Recipe: 2
Calories   2802.4
Fat   267.0g
Cholesterol   199.4mg
Sodium   2626.8mg
Carbohydrates   21.2g
Protein   56.8g

Ingredients

MEAT
1 lb. flank steak, frozen for 30 minutes
MARINADE
1 tsp dry sherry
1 egg
1/4 tsp salt
1 tbsp vegetable oil
1 tbsp cornstarch
SAUCE Ingredients
2 tbsp light soy sauce
2 tbsp dark soy sauce
1 tbsp hoisin sauce
4 tbsp dry sherry
1 tsp sugar
1 tbsp sesame oil
2 tbsp chicken stock
1/2 tsp cornstarch
1/4 tsp black pepper
OTHER Ingredients
1 tsp minced ginger
1/2 tsp minced garlic
7 scallions, cut into 1 1/2 inch pieces
2 tbsp vegetable oil
2 C. vegetable oil

Directions

1. Trim the fat from the steak and cut into 1/8-inch slices.
2. In a bowl, add all the marinade ingredients and mix till well combined.
3. Add the steak slices and refrigerate for about 1/2 hour.
4. In a bowl, dissolve the cornstarch in stock.
5. Add remaining sauce ingredients and mix well.
6. Remove the beef from the bowl.
7. In a wok, heat 2 C. of the oil to 350 degrees F and fry the beef slices till almost done.
8. Transfer the beef in a colander to drain.
9. Remove the oil from wok, leaving 2 tbsp inside.
10. In the same wok, add scallion, ginger and garlic for about 15 seconds.
11. Stir in the sauce ingredients and stir fry for about 15 seconds.
12. Stir in the beef slices and stir fry till heated through.

CLASSIC GRILLED
Teriyaki Salmon

Prep Time: 8 hr
Total Time: 8 hr 12 mins

Servings per Recipe: 4
Calories   272.8
Fat   5.0g
Cholesterol   52.3mg
Sodium   2845.8mg
Carbohydrates   28.6g
Protein   27.6g

Ingredients

1 lb salmon fillet
1 C. teriyaki sauce or 1 C. teriyaki marinade
1/4 C. honey

Directions

1. Get a large bag: Place it in the salmon fillets with teriyaki sauce. Seal the bag and shake it to coat.
2. Before you do anything preheat the grill and grease it.
3. Remove the salmon fillets from the marinade. Cook it on the grill with skin side facing up for 4 min.
4. Rotate the fillet on the other side and cook it for another 4 min. Flip the salmon fillet and brush it with honey. Cook it for 7 min then serve it warm.
5. Enjoy

Tasty Beef Meatballs

Prep Time: 10 mins
Total Time: 35 mins

Servings per Recipe: 6
Calories   174.8
Fat   11.3g
Cholesterol   51.4mg
Sodium   510.6mg
Carbohydrates   2.2g
Protein   14.8g

Ingredients

- 1 lb ground beef
- 1/4 C. teriyaki sauce
- 2 green onions, chopped
- 1/2 tsp grated gingerroot (optional)
- garlic salt

Directions

1. Before you do anything preheat the oven to 350 F.
2. Get a large mixing bowl: Combine in it all the ingredients. Mix them well. Shape the mix into 1 inch meatballs.
3. Place the meatballs on a lined baking sheet. Cook them in the oven for 28 min. Serve them warm.
4. Enjoy.

MONGOLIAN
Potato Quarters

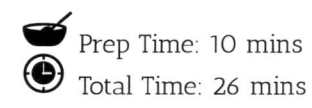

Prep Time: 10 mins
Total Time: 26 mins

Servings per Recipe: 5
Calories 129.9
Fat 2.4g
Cholesterol 6.1mg
Sodium 166.5mg
Carbohydrates 24.7g
Protein 3.0g

Ingredients

1 1/2 lbs red skinned new potatoes (tiny sized, about 10)
1 tbsp butter or 1 tbsp margarine, cut into pieces
1 tbsp bottled teriyaki sauce
1/4 tsp garlic salt, to taste
1/4 tsp italian seasoning, crushed
1 dash black pepper, to taste
1 dash cayenne pepper, to taste
1 tsp fresh rosemary, minced (optional)
sour cream, to garnish (optional)

Directions

1. Clean the potatoes and slice them into quarters. Place it in a microwave proof pan.
2. Add to it the remaining ingredients except for the rosemary and mix them. Put on the lid and microwave them for 17 min on high or until the potatoes becomes soft.
3. Stir in the rosemary then serve your potato casserole warm.
4. Enjoy.

Glazed Swordfish

Prep Time: 15 mins
Total Time: 3 hr 15 mins

Servings per Recipe: 4
Calories   304.9
Fat   13.8g
Cholesterol   66.3mg
Sodium   1533.6mg
Carbohydrates   7.3g
Protein   36.0g

Ingredients

2 tbsp canola oil
1/4 C. chopped white onion
2 -3 minced garlic cloves
1 1/2 tsp grated fresh ginger
1/2 C. teriyaki sauce
1/4 honey
4 (6 oz) center cut swordfish steaks

Directions

1. Place a saucepan over medium heat. Heat the oil in it. Cook in it the onion, garlic and ginger for 4 min.
2. Stir in the honey with teriyaki sauce. Cook them until they start boiling while stirring all the time. Lower the heat and cook them for 3 min.
3. Place the sauce aside to lose heat. Reserve 1/4 of the sauce.
4. Get a large zip lock bag: Place in it the remaining sauce with swordfish steaks. Seal the bag and shake it to coat. Place it in the fridge for 2 h 30.
5. Before you do anything preheat the grill for 6 min and grease it.
6. Drain the swordfish from the sauce. Cook the swordfish steaks in the grill for 5 min on each side.
7. Remove the steaks from the grill and spray them with a cooking spray. Wipe the grill clean.
8. Cook the swordfish for 4 min on each side with basting them with the reserved sauce. Serve your swordfish steaks warm.
9. Enjoy.

TIPSY MAHI MAHI
Teriyaki With Fruity Jalapeno Salsa

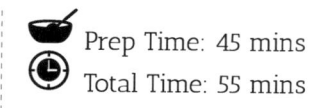

Prep Time: 45 mins
Total Time: 55 mins

Servings per Recipe: 4
Calories 324.5
Fat 8.4g
Cholesterol 8.4g
Sodium 148.9mg
Carbohydrates 1297.8mg
Protein 17.4g

Ingredients

Salsa:
1 large ripe mango
1/4 C. finely chopped red onion
1 tbsp vegetable oil
1 tbsp fresh lime juice
1 tbsp finely chopped of fresh mint
1 tsp minced jalapeno pepper, with seeds
1/4 tsp kosher salt
Marinade:
1/4 C. soy sauce
1/4 C. broth
1 tbsp vegetable oil
1 tbsp light brown sugar
1 tsp grated fresh ginger
1 tsp minced garlic
4 mahi mahi fillets, about 6 oz. each and 1 inch thick
vegetable oil

Directions

1. To make the salsa:
2. Peel the mango and cut it into 1/4 inch dices.
3. Get a serving bowl: Toss it in the mango dices with the rest of the ingredients. Place it in the fridge until ready to serve.
4. To make the mahi mahi fillets:
5. Get a small bowl: Mix in it the soy sauce, broth, vegetable oil, light brown sugar, fresh ginger, and minced garlic to make the marinade.
6. Get a large zip lock bag: Place in it the mahi mahi fillets and marinade. Seal it and shake it to coat. Place it in the fridge for 28 min.
7. Before you do anything preheat the grill and grease it.
8. Drain the mahi mahi fillet. Spray them on both sides with a cooking spray. Cook them in the grill for 4 to 6 min on each side.
9. Serve your teriyaki mahi mahi fillets with the jalapeno salsa.
10. Enjoy.

Mongolian Teriyaki Meat

Prep Time: 15 mins
Total Time: 25 mins

Servings per Recipe: 10
Calories   980.7
Fat   96.5g
Cholesterol   134.8mg
Sodium   995.8mg
Carbohydrates   12.3g
Protein   12.4g

Ingredients

3 - 4 lbs beef or 3 - 4 lbs chicken
Sauce:
2/3 C. shoyu (Asian soy sauce)
1/2 C. sugar
2 tbsp broth
3 garlic cloves, minced
1 inch piece ginger, crushed
3 green onions (chopped fine)
1 tsp Chinese five spice powder (optional)

Directions

1. Get a large zip lock bag: Combine in it all the ingredients. Seal the bag and shake it to coat. Place it in the fridge for 5 h to an overnight.
2. Before you do anything preheat the oven to 325 F.
3. Pour the mix into a roasting casserole dish. Cook it in the oven for 1 h 10 min. Serve your meat casserole warm.
4. Enjoy.

ORIENTAL
Tuna Steaks

Prep Time: 2 hr
Total Time: 2 hr 12 mins

Servings per Recipe: 4
Calories   179.4
Fat   10.1g
Cholesterol   0.0mg
Sodium   1011.1mg
Carbohydrates   14.2g
Protein   2.1g

Ingredients

1/4 C. soy sauce
3 tbsp brown sugar
3 tbsp olive oil
2 tbsp white wine vinegar
2 tbsp chicken broth
2 tbsp unsweetened pineapple juice

3 cloves garlic, minced
1 tsp ground ginger
1/8 tsp black pepper
4 tuna steaks (about 6 oz. each)

Directions

1. Get a large mixing bowl: Mix in it all the ingredients except for the tuna steaks to make the marinade.
2. Get a large zip lock bag: Place in it the tuna steaks with marinade. Seal it and shake it to coat. Place it in the fridge for 1 h 20 min.
3. Before you do anything preheat the grill and grease it.
4. Remove the tuna steaks from the marinade and grill them for 7 min on each side while basting them with the marinade.
5. Serve your steaks warm.
6. Enjoy.

Chicken Kabobs II

Prep Time: 1 hr 30 mins
Total Time: 2 hr

Servings per Recipe: 24
Calories 93.7
Fat 5.0g
Cholesterol 31.4mg
Sodium 717.1mg
Carbohydrates 3.0g
Protein 8.5g

Ingredients

2 lbs boneless skinless chicken thighs
1 tbsp sesame seeds, toasted
MARINADE
15 oz teriyaki sauce
6 tbsp sesame oil
1/4 tsp minced garlic
1 lemon, juice of
1 tbsp Splenda granular (sugar substitute)

Directions

1. Place some bamboo skewers in some water to some for at least 1 h 10 min.
2. Get a large mixing bowl: Combine in it all the marinade ingredients and whisk them well.
3. Cut the chicken thighs into stripes and dip them into the marinade. Cover the bowl with a piece of foil and place it in the fridge for 1 h 30 min.
4. Before you do anything preheat the oven to 375 F.
5. Thread each chicken thigh strip into a bamboo skewer. Lay them on a lined up baking sheet. Cook them in the oven for 32 min.
6. Sprinkle the sesame seeds over the skewers. Serve them warm.
7. Enjoy.

TILAPIA FILLETS
with Teriyaki Sauce

Prep Time: 5 mins
Total Time: 15 mins

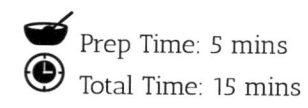

Servings per Recipe: 5	
Calories	245.6
Fat	4.8g
Cholesterol	62.5mg
Sodium	1680.0mg
Carbohydrates	23.3g
Protein	28.1g

Ingredients

- 1 tbsp oil
- 5 tilapia fillets
- 1/2 C. brown sugar
- 1/4 C. seasoned rice wine vinegar
- 1/2 C. soy sauce
- 1 tsp fresh ginger, grated
- 1/2 tsp garlic, minced

Directions

1. Place a large skillet over medium heat. Add the oil and heat it. Lay in it the tilapia Fillets.
2. Get a mixing bowl: Mix in it the remaining ingredients to make the sauce. Pour the sauce all over the tilapia. Cook them until the fish is done and sauce is thick.
3. Serve your tilapia fillets with teriyaki sauce warm.
4. Enjoy.

Glazed Salmon Fillets with Orzo

🥣 Prep Time: 15 mins
🕐 Total Time: 25 mins

Servings per Recipe: 4
Calories   849.7
Fat   31.3g
Cholesterol   153.6mg
Sodium   3001.4mg
Carbohydrates   55.8g
Protein   81.8g

Ingredients

- 4 salmon fillets (2 lbs total)
- 1 oz canola oil
- 1 oz soy sauce
- 8 oz teriyaki sauce
- 8 oz orzo pasta, precooked
- 2 garlic cloves, minced
- 2 tbsp olive oil, combined with garlic
- 1/2 C. red bell pepper, diced
- 1/3 C. parmesan cheese
- 8 oz spinach, julienned

Directions

1. Before you do anything preheat the grill and grease it.
2. Coat the salmon fillets with soy sauce and brush them with the oil. Cook them in the grill for 4 min on each side.
3. Brush the salmon fillets with 2 oz of teriyaki glaze. Cook them for 3 min on each side.
4. Cook the orzo according to the directions on the package.
5. Place a large skillet over medium heat. Heat the oil in it. Add the garlic with peppers and orzo. Cook them for 2 min.
6. Stir in the cheese until it melts. Turn off the heat and add the spinach. Stir them several times until the spinach wilts.
7. Serve your orzo with the glazed salmon fillets and the remaining teriyaki sauce.
8. Enjoy.

MONGOLIAN
Burgers

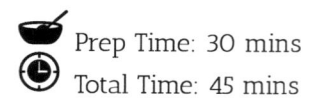

🥣 Prep Time: 30 mins
🕐 Total Time: 45 mins

Servings per Recipe: 4
Calories   402.7
Fat   11.1g
Cholesterol   93.0mg
Sodium   31740.4mg
Carbohydrates   62.8g
Protein   213.5g

Ingredients

1/2 tbsp peanut oil
1/2 C. onion (purple)
1 C. zucchini
1/2 C. red bell pepper
2 eggs
1/2 tsp ginger (ground)
1/2 tsp cumin
1/4 C. soy sauce
1/4 C. teriyaki sauce
1/4 C. walnut pieces
1 1/2 C. brown rice (cooked)

Directions

1. Before you do anything heat the oven on 350 F.
2. Chop the bell pepper with zucchini until they become fine. Mince the onion.
3. Place a large skillet on medium heat. Add the oil and heat it. Stir in the onion and cook it for 6 min.
4. Stir in the chopped zucchini with bell pepper to the onion. Cook them for 16 min while stirring occasionally. Turn off the heat and allow the mix to lose heat.
5. Get a mixing bowl: Add the eggs and beat them. Stir in the onion mix with ginger, cumin, soy sauce, teriyaki sauce, walnuts and cooked rice. Mix them well. Shape the mix into 4 burgers.
6. Place the burgers on the baking pan. Cook them in the oven for 8 min on each side.
7. Assemble your burgers with your favorite toppings. Serve them right away.
8. Enjoy.

ENJOY THE RECIPES?

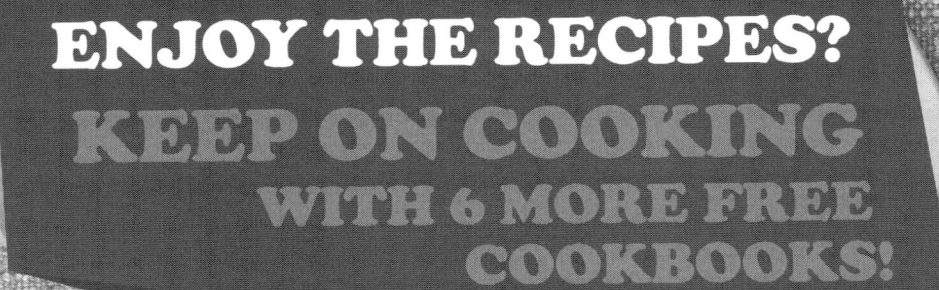

KEEP ON COOKING WITH 6 MORE FREE COOKBOOKS!

Click the link below and simply enter your email address to join the club and receive your 6 cookbooks.

http://booksumo.com/magnet

https://www.instagram.com/booksumopress/

https://www.facebook.com/booksumo/

Printed in Great Britain
by Amazon